GOLF RULES ILLUSTRATED

THE CALLAWAY GOLFER

CALLAWAY EDITIONS

64 Bedford Street New York, NY 10014

Printed in Hong Kong by Palace Press International

First Edition

10 9 8 7 6 5 4 3 2 1

Library of Congress Catalog Card Information Available

ISBN 0-935112-51-0

A NOTE ON THE TYPE: The text was set in *Gill Sans*, designed by Eric Gill 1927-1930.
Cover titling and the sans serif throughout the book is *Griffith Gothic*, a revival of C.H.
Griffith's 1937 Bell Gothic Mergenthaler original, redrawn by Tobias Frere-Jones in 1997.

EDITOR-IN-CHIEF: Nicholas Callaway   EDITOR, THE CALLAWAY GOLFER: Edward Brash
ASSOCIATE PUBLISHER: Paula Litzky   DIRECTOR OF PRODUCTION: True Sims
ART DIRECTOR & DESIGNER: Jennifer Wagner   EDITOR: Christopher Steighner

ALSO AVAILABLE FROM THE CALLAWAY GOLFER:

Breaking 90 with Johnny Miller
The Story of American Golf, Volume One: 1888-1941

VISIT CALLAWAY EDITIONS AT WWW.CALLAWAY.COM

GOLF RULES ILLUSTRATED

CALLAWAY EDITIONS

New York
2000

GOLF RULES ILLUSTRATED

CHAPTER ONE

HOW TO USE THIS BOOK   PLAY IT AS IT LIES
DISTINCTION BETWEEN THE TWO KINDS OF PENALTIES
DISTINCTION BETWEEN STROKE PLAY AND MATCH PLAY
WHY WE NEED THE RULES

BEFORE
YOU BEGIN

Rules Basics

This is a book for golfers who believe that they would enjoy golf more if they understood the rules a little better—or a lot better—than they do now.

The rules appeal to our sense of fair play. They not only stiffen golf's challenge but hand the golfer an occasional break as well. Ignorance of a rule can cause embarrassment on the course, or worse, the loss of a precious stroke or two on the scorecard. It doesn't matter whether it's a money match, a formal tournament, a round against par, or a round against a golfer's previous performance. The rules play a vital role in protecting golf's challenge. This book will help you gain a finer appreciation for this challenge, which is at the heart of the game.

Looking at the history of the rules, you can follow this challenge all the way back to 1744, when The Honourable Company of Edinburgh Golfers in Scotland compiled the first formalized set of rules in 1744. Over time these rules evolved and the Royal and Ancient Golf Club of St. Andrews, Scotland, established itself as the central arbiter and keeper of the rules. Toward the end of the 19th century, Americans took up the game and its popularity here grew so quickly that by the early 1900s, golf's power seat began to shift. The United States Golf Association was formed in 1894 and quickly gained credibility as a reputable institution in its own right. By the 1950s, the U.S.G.A. and the R&A were working in cooperation to revise and regulate the rules for golf around the world. Today these joint superpowers still reign, and supply us with revised rules every four years in the booklet the Rules of Golf as well as thousands of "decisions," which are golf's equivalent of law-book precedents.

In fact, because the Rules of Golf is a product of years of revision and committee decisions, it is a complicated, multilayered document. Its language and structure can resemble a legal contract's. On the other hand, once you learn how to use this book, you will have a friendly guide for the sometimes gnarly forest of the rules. *Golf Rules Illustrated* is not intended to replace the official rule book but to provide a valuable and helpful companion to it. The two are meant to work in tandem. This book will familiarize you enough with the basic rules so that eventually you will feel comfortable looking up even the most complex question on your own in the rule book.

You will need an up-to-date copy of the Rules of Golf at all times. You can purchase one easily enough, for one dollar, by calling 1-800-755-0293 or by visiting the U.S.G.A. on the Internet at *www.usga.org*. At this Web site you can also access the full text of the rules, complete with hypertext links that connect related rules to each other, and search by keyword.

The best way to use *Golf Rules Illustrated* is to read it first straight through. Then, tuck it in your golf bag along with your rule book and refer to it whenever a specific question arises. We have designed it as a pocket reference, with many special features to help you pinpoint the answer you need on the spot. First, there is a detailed Table of Contents. When you have a question about a specific topic, such as water hazards, you can just scan the Table of Contents and then go to the section on that topic. For easy reference, each topic is always found in red type at the top of each page. Within the body text, each main topic appears in red type, and in gray type is the penalty that is the consequence of the situation described. Instructive quotations appear in red type in the margins. At the end of each chapter appears a chart summing up the chapter's main points.

Another distinguishing feature of this book are Greg Clarke's memorable illustrations, which appear throughout to help you visualize the major rules procedures. Scottie IV, our imaginary mascot-guide, acts out in pictures the right ways to proceed on the course. Scottie, however, occasionally indulges in dramatic behavior (to make a point) that you should not imitate: such as using scuba gear in a water hazard. These transgressions seem obvious enough not to require further comment.

Trying to memorize or comprehend the entire Rules of Golf is beyond most of us. It makes more sense to work our way under the skin of the rules, starting with the most common trouble situations and working in from there. That is the way we have organized this book. Since your first encounters with the rules are likely to involve an out-of-bounds ball, a lost ball, a water hazard, or a lateral water hazard, we cover these situations first, in the following chapter. A little less common but still important are unplayable lies, obstructions, ground under repair, and casual water, all in Chapter 3. Next come a couple chapters on general situations you will encounter on the course between tee and green. Then you're likely to have questions about life in the bunker (Chapter 6). Finally, when you get to the green, you will have etiquette and rules queries (Chapter 7).

After you've learned these most essential rules, the book provides three chapters that offer general advice on how to approach the rule book itself. In Chapter 8, there are tips on how to use the rule book to anticipate rules run-ins by examining a hole in advance. Chapter 9 tells how to personalize your copy of the rule book. And, Chapter 10 offers counsel on how best to give rules advice in on-course situations. By the time you reach this last chapter, you should be a more skilled practitioner of the rules' arcane science.

Just as every science has its founding principles, the rules have several underlying truths that you should recognize from the beginning. First of all, there is the classic and central mandate: Play it as it lies (Rule 13). This is what drives the game—what provides the challenge as well as the factor of random chance. You can never be wrong with the rules if you just play it as it lies. No matter where your ball lands—in water, on a rock, in a tree, on a cart path—this is always an option. Since it is ever present, the Rules of Golf does not repeat this and neither does this book when discussing specific rules. Just remember that it's always available if you would like to use it.

"If a Ball be Stop'd by any person, Horse, Dog or any thing else, the Ball so Stop'd Must be played where it lyes."—from the original 1744 R&A rules

Secondly, it's important to realize the distinction between the two kinds of penalties: There is the penalty for a shot that ends poorly, and then there is the penalty for the breach of a rule. For instance, if you hit into a water hazard—a shot that ends poorly— you incur a one-stroke penalty. But if you ignore that penalty stroke or you don't follow the proper procedure to put your ball back in play, you are assessed a two-stroke penalty for breach of Rule 26-1. It is this second, more severe, breach-of-rule penalty that is printed in capital letters at the end of each rule in the official rule book. This can be misleading since your eye is naturally drawn to this penalty first and your inclination may be to follow it automatically. But you have to read the complete text of the rule in order to find the correct penalty. Alternately, this book highlights in gray type the penalties the rules assess you for shots that end poorly so you can get the most important information immediately when needed. If you follow these rules, you will never be hit with the more severe type of penalty.

Another recurring cause of confusion in the Rules of Golf involves the distinction between stroke play and match play. Depending on the situation, the rules mete out different penalties for the different kinds of play. Basically all you need to remember is that stroke play is the game that the average golfer plays most often so it is the stroke-play penalties that most frequently apply to your game. Generally match play is used in tournaments. In match play, whoever finishes a hole in the fewest strokes wins that hole. A match is won by a player who is leading by a number of holes greater than the number of holes remaining to be played. This book focuses on penalties for stroke play since that is more common, and match-play penalties are given secondarily.

Forming the foundation of the rules also are the components that begin and end the main text of the rule book: the definitions and the index. The definitions at the front of the rule book cover ten or so pages; you should read them in their entirety. Even though you may know exactly what a bunker is, it's only when you read this term's definition that you will learn that a grassy area within a bunker is not considered part of a bunker. The index, which covers eighteen pages at the end of the most recent edition of the Rules of Golf, provides a key to finding a specific rule in question. But, keep in mind that you may need to visit several sites before you get the full answer. For instance, if you look up the entry for "Ball, searching for," the rule first cited by the index—Rule 12-1—it will not tell you how long you may spend searching for the ball. In order to find that you must look up "Lost Ball" in the index, which directs you to the definition for that term in the front of the book.

After this kind of roundabout referencing in the rule book, you may start to wonder why we need the rules. The rules, when all is said and done, are nothing more than an answer to the question: How difficult—how great a challenge—should the game of golf be? There are hundreds of shortcuts and sidesteps available to reduce the game's challenge, from mulligans to preferred lies to the wild whiff that was "just a practice swing." It is human nature to beg these forms of forgiveness. But isn't there a different satisfaction that comes from refusing to take a mulligan, playing a poorly hit drive from where it lies, and stroking it 220 morally pure yards toward the green?

Through the centuries the typical rules maker has not been a scientist but a moralist. He has stared into players' souls and recognized the golfer's instinctive sense of entitlement—to the perfect lie, to the favorable bounce, to a firm and level piece of turf to stand on. Aware that these impulses toward individual privilege would, if indulged, destroy golf's beautifully calibrated balance between frustration and well-deserved reward, the mind of the rules maker has built, clause by clause, a code of precise limits that yields a sublime sporting experience.

A century ago Mark Twain said that golf was a game played "with implements ill-suited to the purpose." He would surely give a different appraisal in today's realm of super high-tech equipment. Again and again technology has been accused of eroding the challenge that defines the game. Meanwhile, the turf-grass on greens and fairways continues to be groomed closer and closer to perfection. The challenge of the game endures, but its early hardships have been greatly smoothed over. If there were ever a time in the game's history when the rules could make their move to take their rightful place at the heart of the game, the early years of this new century are that time.

RULE

You can carry with you a maximum of fourteen clubs.

At the 1st tee, the order of play is determined by a chance method such as drawing lots. At the other tees whoever has the lowest score from the previous hole plays first.

Only at the tee, if a ball is nudged off its perch during address, there is no penalty and the player re-tees. If the ball falls after the player has started to swing, however, the stroke is counted.

Remember you are going to have to search for the ball if it goes astray and that there is a time limit on this search. So keep your eyes open for the ball's landing spot after you've teed off.

GETTING IN TROUBLE

The Four Most Common Situations

"A BALL IS *OUT OF BOUNDS* WHEN ALL OF IT LIES *OUT OF BOUNDS*." — RULE 27, DEFINITIONS

Where the rules and everyday golf most often intersect is when a player loses a ball, hits it out of bounds, or hits it into a water hazard. When one of these events occurs, a player may find it hard to recall what procedure to follow. Hitting a mulligan or a "do-over" is not the answer; a mulligan, or any of its many variations, is in violation of the rules. Here's what the rules intend for you to do.

Golfers lose balls and hit them out of bounds all the time. Both situations are treated under the same rule, Rule 27, Ball Lost or Out of Bounds; Provisional Ball.

Both are assessed the same severe penalty. It's called the stroke-and-distance penalty. To understand what it means, let's first walk through a lost-ball scenario. You hook your tee shot into woods that are in bounds but are littered with sticks, undergrowth, tree roots, and fallen leaves. You know these woods. Your ball will not be found. You go through the motions of a search but turn up nothing. The rules allow only five minutes for searching; once that time has passed, your ball is considered lost.

At this point Rule 27 assesses a stroke and distance. Stroke means that you incur a one-stroke penalty for having lost a ball. Distance means that in order to remedy the situation, you must return to the spot from which you last hit, and then hit again. This is your relief. (In rules talk, relief means the proper method by which you should get yourself back into the game after a foul-up—it's relief from whatever obstacle or mishap assails you.) So, stroke *and* distance indicates both your penalty (one stroke) and your relief procedure (return to the last spot).

STROKE-AND-DISTANCE PROCEDURE
FOR OUT-OF-BOUNDS OR LOST BALL

RULE

27

STEP 1

FIRST STROKE INTO THE WOODS
BALL IS LOST OR O.B.

STEP 2

BACK TO TEE

PENALTY STROKE MAKES TWO
PLUS DISTANCE BACK TO TEE

HITTING THREE

RULE

When people speak of distance in terms of the rules, they are referring to how far back you have to walk (or ride) to reach the spot from which your ball was last struck. In some penalty situations, such as water hazards, the rules tell you that you can drop near where you ran into the trouble, so in these cases there is no distance penalty. But with lost balls or with out-of-bounds balls, you are assessed both stroke and distance, and have to go back to your last spot and then drop. Pushing you back on the course almost always means adding another stroke to your score (in addition to the penalty stroke). In this way you could think of stroke and distance as the equivalent of a two-stroke penalty. To mentally figure your score, you could say: one into the woods, two back to the last spot, hitting three.

There is a way, however, to reduce the burden of this penalty. It is the provisional ball. The trip back to your last spot not only delays play but can also damage your self-confidence, which in turn endangers your second try. To avoid this, you can, upon watching your ball disappear, announce that you intend to play a provisional. Once your fellow players are done teeing off, hit your second ball, which with luck will find a decent fairway lie. Figure it this way: one into the woods, two as a penalty stroke, hitting three from the tee as a provisional. When you find where your provisional is lying, you will be about to hit your fourth shot. It's the same stroke and distance as described above; the difference is that the provisional eliminates the need to make the trip back to the tee if you don't find your first ball. Psychologically it improves your disposition; it's reassuring to know you have a backup plan already in place. Hitting a provisional is something you can do anywhere on the course, not just on the tee, whenever you think you have lost a ball or whenever you think you have hit one out-of-bounds. It works the same in both situations.

Unless you are an unusually accurate player, you should expect to hit at least one provisional ball every round or two. If you happen to hit a dicey shot from the tee (and you aren't last in your group to hit), state right away that you "probably need to hit a provisional." A minute later, when the last golfer in the group has teed off, you can expect that not one single member of the group will have remembered your predicament or your mention of the provisional, thus requiring you to raise your voice a bit as you tee up the provisional ball. And remember to hit a ball marked differently from the first one for your provisional; otherwise you could find the two of them lying ten feet apart

"IF THE ORIGINAL BALL IS NEITHER *LOST* NOR *OUT OF BOUNDS*, THE PLAYER SHALL ABANDON THE *PROVISIONAL BALL* AND CONTINUE PLAY WITH THE ORIGINAL BALL."
—RULE 27-2C

in the rough and not know which is your ball in play—that would make both of them lost balls.

Now let's walk through the procedure for a ball out-of-bounds, going back to the tee again. You hook your drive into woods along the fairway and past the line of white stakes that mark the hole's boundary. Your ball is out of bounds. O.B. The penalty is just the same as that for lost balls—stroke and distance. You must count a penalty stroke, go back to the spot from which you first struck, and hit again. Or hit a provisional.

The fact that both lost balls and out-of-bounds balls have the same penalty and relief procedure gives us a hint into the logic behind the rules. The idea is that it's just as bad to lose your ball as it is to hit it completely off the course. By placing lost balls in the same category as out-of-bounds balls, the rule makers are emphasizing the importance of paying attention to where your ball lands and to understanding the lay of the course. This is not just good for the individual golfer but good for the whole course, since being able to quickly find or play your ball keeps course traffic moving.

The next penalty situation in which golfers most commonly find themselves is the water hazard. When you lose one in the water, you feel that you've failed a little test that the course architect designed. Perhaps it is because of this that the penalty is not quite as harsh as for balls lost outside of a hazard or for O.B. balls. It's almost as if you're expected to hit into water at least some of the time; even the pros do it. So the rule book treats you a little better than if you lose a ball or hit it out-of-bounds.

Say on a 190-yard par-3 there's a stream fronting the green. Your wind-tossed tee shot is short, finds the stream, and the ball disappears. It is lost in a water hazard and Rule 26, Water Hazards (Including Lateral Water Hazards), applies. Accordingly, you approach the stream and need to estimate the point where your ball crossed into the area of the hazard. Note that this is the point your ball enters the airspace of the hazard, not the point where your ball sinks

RELIEF OPTIONS FOR WATER HAZARDS

RULE

26

into the water. You form an imaginary line connecting the hole and this point of entry. You must drop a new ball along this line. You can drop as far back from the hazard as you wish as long as you stay along this line. This is good to remember because sometimes moving farther back improves the situation. It can put you in better range to take a full swing with your wedge or 9-iron rather than a riskier three-quarters swing, or it can give you a better look at the hole. If you wish, you could instead go all the way back to the tee and hit from there, but it's rare that doing that helps you.

In any case, there is also a one-stroke penalty. You can calculate your score this way: one in the stream, two out of the water, hitting three. You've taken a knock, but at least you don't have to return to the tee. If you've been practicing your short game and putting (like you should be), you may be able to get away with nothing worse than a bogey.

Sometimes, if the water is shallow, or if you're feeling a bit adventurous, you may think you can make a decent shot by striking the ball from out of the water. This would be playing the ball as it lies. There's no penalty for doing this so go for it. However, you are not allowed to ground your club—that is, you cannot prepare your shot by putting your clubhead into the water next to the ball. You must hit it in one fell swoop, letting your club enter the water only as you swing.

But, what if you hit into a body of water that runs lengthwise alongside the fairway, a creek or stream that lies parallel to the right- or left-side boundary of the hole? There is really no way to drop *behind* this kind of hazard. Hence it is classified as a different species of water hazard—the lateral water hazard—and it has slightly different relief options. It is important to recognize the difference between the two types because the lateral hazard can save you from having to move backward on the course. With a lateral hazard you still must take a one-stroke penalty. But you do have the choice of dropping a new ball near the point at which your ball crossed into the hazard. To do this, first determine this point, then drop within two club-lengths of that spot (but no closer to the hole).

Your other option is to drop on the farside of the lateral hazard, which is the bank of the creek that's farther from the fairway. Again this spot cannot be closer to the hole than the point at which your ball crossed into the hazard. The rare case that this farside drop would be preferable is if it gives you a better angle or a better distance from which to hit. You also have the

"THE MARGIN OF A *WATER HAZARD* EXTENDS VERTICALLY UPWARDS AND DOWNWARDS."
—RULE 26, DEFINITIONS

PLAY IT AS IT LIES
NO PENALTY

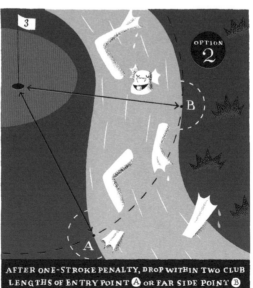

AFTER ONE-STROKE PENALTY, DROP WITHIN TWO CLUB
LENGTHS OF ENTRY POINT **A** OR FAR SIDE POINT **B**

two other options that are standard for a regular water hazard. You could take stroke and distance, returning to the spot from which you last hit. Or you could connect a line between the hole and the ball's point of entry and drop as far back as you wish along this line but no nearer the hole. These last two options are very rarely preferable. Only certain strange course layouts would make either of these options desirable for a lateral hazard.

If you are not sure what kind of water hazard it is that you've hit into, you can tell from the course markings. Lateral hazards have red stakes while regular water hazards have yellow stakes. You might want to develop your own mnemonic device to remember these colors. Here's one suggestion: The Red River doesn't flow to Yellowstone Lake. You can think of it like this: Red River is a long waterway that flows alongside the hole (lateral hazard), whereas Yellowstone Lake is a calmer, larger body of water that spans the fairway (regular water hazard).

You may come across an area that is marked as a lateral water hazard but that contains no discernible water, creek, or swampland. These are *wetlands*, a catchall term that course committees use even though some of the lands in question are truly wet only ten or fifteen days a year. The committee is trying to make life easier for players by keeping them from creeping through swampy lowlands. The committee is also trying, in some cases, to protect a fragile environment. The most logical option would be to designate these areas as out of bounds, but the makers of the local rules feel that would exact too heavy a penalty. So, the solution is the lateral hazard designation, which exacts a stroke but not distance.

RULES TO REMEMBER: **EVERYDAY TROUBLES**

SITUATION	COURSE MARKER	PENALTY	RELIEF	RULE
LOST BALL	NONE	ONE STROKE	RETURN TO LAST SPOT (DISTANCE)	27
OUT OF BOUNDS	WHITE STAKES	ONE STROKE	RETURN TO LAST SPOT (DISTANCE)	27
WATER HAZARD	YELLOW STAKES	ONE STROKE	BEST OPTION: DROP BEHIND HAZARD	26
LATERAL HAZARD	RED STAKES	ONE STROKE	BEST OPTION: DROP NEAR POINT OF BALL'S CROSSING	26

FINDING A CLEAR PATH

Relief from Unintended Obstacles

There are times when a well-struck ball does not achieve the bonny lie it deserves. It comes to rest on or near an obstacle that is not part of the course architect's plan for creating a challenging hole. Rather, these obstacles are man-made or natural ones that occur either by accident or because of the practical necessities of course maintenance. Since they are unintended, the rules governing them are forgiving. When you hit into a bunker or a water hazard, you are supposed to have some trouble. When you hit a ball out of bounds or lose a ball, you are supposed to have more trouble. But when you hit into an area made hard by maintenance vehicle traffic, the rules let you off. One of the great advantages of learning the rule book is to know when to invoke rules that can come to your aid. Here is an explanation of the most important rules governing these unintended obstacles.

Let's say that your ball comes to rest perilously close to a tree or its roots, or on a brick-hard pathway that is much-traveled but not paved, or on a hillside that erosion has left carpeted with stones or an exposed rock outcropping. Technically, you can hit it just as if it were on a decent lie in the fairway. But the reality is that if you tried, you might damage your score, your club, or worse, injure yourself.

The rules contain a perfectly fine alternative to hitting risky shots from rocky lies or from those baked clay surfaces called hardpan. That alternative is to declare your ball unplayable under Rule 28, Ball Unplayable. Once you've told the other players that your ball is unplayable, you can, under penalty of one stroke, choose between three options for relief: 1) You can return to the spot from which you just played and re-hit. 2) You can drop within two club-lengths of the unplayable spot but not nearer the hole and play your next shot. 3) You form an imaginary line between the hole and the unplayable spot, then drop anywhere behind the unplayable spot along the extension of this line. You can do this anywhere on the course—except in a bunker, where there are some restrictions, or in a water hazard, where this option is not available to you.

OPTION
1

TO LAST
SPOT
PLAYED

TAKE ONE-STROKE PENALTY, RETURN TO SPOT FROM WHICH YOU JUST PLAYED AND RE-HIT

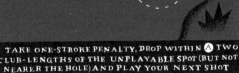

TAKE ONE-STROKE PENALTY, DROP WITHIN (A) TWO
CLUB-LENGTHS OF THE UNPLAYABLE SPOT (BUT NOT
NEARER THE HOLE) AND PLAY YOUR NEXT SHOT

TAKE ONE-STROKE PENALTY, FORM IMAGINARY LINE
BETWEEN HOLE & UNPLAYABLE SPOT, THEN DROP
BEHIND SPOT ALONG EXTENSION OF THIS LINE

RELIEF OPTIONS FOR
UNPLAYABLE BALL

RULE

28

Golfers occasionally encounter lies that aren't really unplayable, but are encumbered by movable natural objects like leaves, twigs, fallen branches, pebbles, or evidence of wildlife. If your ball lands in such a spot, this situation is covered by Rule 23, Loose Impediments. Unless you're within a bunker, you can obtain relief without any penalty. Just brush or kick away the bothersome objects, but if you disturb your ball you will incur a one-stroke penalty (we'll discuss this penalty more in Chapter 5). Something that is growing and planted in the ground, such as a root, a bush, or reeds, does not qualify as a loose impediment and cannot be moved.

"SAND AND LOOSE SOIL ARE LOOSE IMPEDIMENTS ON THE PUTTING GREEN BUT NOT ELSEWHERE"
—RULE 23, DEFINITION

Perhaps your ball finds itself attracted to objects bigger than pebbles or pinecones, objects that are usually man-made and that the rules term "movable or immovable obstructions." Your ball may have come to rest on a footbridge or near a landscaping tractor. You may find you can't take a normal swing without hitting a sign or that you can't take a normal stance without tripping over a sprinkler head. Again, as long as you're not in a bunker or water hazard, the rules give you free relief, this time under Rule 24, Obstructions. If you can move the object, it's okay to do so.

If the object is harder to move, like a cement walkway, you have to first figure what is the nearest playable point on the course—with a walkway this would be the spot right where the grass begins and the cement stops. Then you can drop the ball anywhere within one club-length of this point but not in a position that is closer to

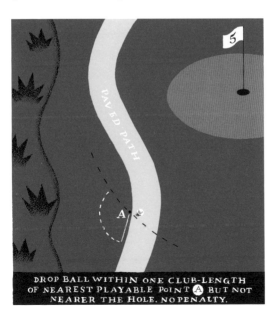

DROP BALL WITHIN ONE CLUB-LENGTH OF NEAREST PLAYABLE POINT **A** BUT NOT NEARER THE HOLE. NO PENALTY.

the hole. On a paved pathway that runs alongside the hole, if your ball lies closer to the farside of the pathway, you have to drop on the farside. Remember that it's relief you're accepting, not an invitation to improve your lie.

It may seem that the stakes and fences that line a hole's boundary should be considered obstructions since they're artificial. But, since they mark the off-limits area of the course, these objects are off-limits themselves. If you hit next to one, you can't get free relief. The rules are, in effect, saying that you should not have hit so close to the O.B. line in the first place, so don't expect any special concessions here.

There's yet another rule that will give you free relief from the unexpected obstacles your ball may encounter—Rule 25, Abnormal Ground Conditions. This rule covers ground under repair, casual water, and embedded balls. Ground under repair is often clearly marked by the maintenance crew, with a line of white encircling it or some sort of sign telling players that a certain area is a work in progress. This could be a place where new sod is being installed, where an irrigation system is being dug, or where bunkers are being repaired. However, it sometimes happens that certain areas qualify as ground under repair even though they may not be marked as such. These are instances in which the course crew has disrupted the land in a spot temporarily, and it's clear that they intend to fix it soon. Maybe a mower has inflicted obvious damage on a part of the green. The grounds crew hasn't bothered to mark this since it will be taken care of soon. But if your ball lands in this area, you can get relief. The procedure for relief from such an area and from any ground under repair is the same as that for an immovable obstruction, explained above. Find the nearest point that is free of the problem and then drop the ball within one club-length, but not nearer to the hole.

"A BALL IS IN *GROUND UNDER REPAIR* WHEN IT LIES IN OR ANY PART OF IT TOUCHES THE *GROUND UNDER REPAIR*."
—RULE 25, DEFINITIONS

You should follow this same procedure if you end up in what the rule book calls casual water. This is water that the course did not intend to have on the course, but which Mother Nature has casually dispensed on her own. It could be a puddle or even a thin film of standing water that follows a rainstorm or a malfunction of the irrigation system. If it's a puddle within a bunker, you can drop within the bunker without penalty, or you can take a penalty stroke and drop anywhere behind the bunker in line with the spot of the original lie.

Every now and then a part of the course starts sucking down your ball like quicksand. Usually due to an abundance of rainfall and to poor drainage, some patches of the course can become spongelike. When your ball lands there, it sinks so deeply into the ground that it would be impossible to hit. This is covered under Rule 25-2, Embedded Ball. You are allowed to lift the ball, clean off the muck, and drop it as near as possible to where it was plugged. There is no penalty. However you can take this free drop only if the soft spot is found where the grass is cut at fairway height or less—basically either on the fairway or the green. If the muck is in the rough, where the grass is tall, you get no free relief.

RULE

If your ball hits a natural or man-made object and ricochets off, **your ball should be played wherever it lands, without penalty.**

19-1

If your ball hits another player's ball at rest on the course, there is no penalty for either person involved. The other player's ball gets re-placed and you must play your ball from wherever it happens to end up.

18-5

If you play a stroke and your ball accidentally hits your body, your golf cart, your bag, your partner (as opposed to your opponent), your partner's bag, or your own or your partner's caddy, **you incur a two-stroke penalty and must play the ball from where it ended up. In match play, you lose the hole.**

19-2

If you play a stroke and it hits your opponent, or any piece of your opponent's equipment, or your opponent's caddy, you can either replay the stroke or play the ball as it lies without penalty.

19-3

THE PITFALL	THE WAY OUT
UNPLAYABLE BALL	ONE PENALTY STROKE AND EITHER:
	1 REPLACE AS NEAR AS POSSIBLE, OR
	2 DROP WITHIN TWO CLUB-LENGTHS, OR
	3 DROP ANYWHERE BACK ON COURSE IN LINE WITH HOLE
LOOSE IMPEDIMENTS	NO PENALTY, BRUSH THEM AWAY
MOVABLE OBSTRUCTIONS	NO PENALTY, REMOVE THEM
IMMOVABLE OBSTRUCTIONS	NO PENALTY, DROP WITHIN ONE CLUB-LENGTH
GROUND UNDER REPAIR	NO PENALTY, DROP WITHIN ONE CLUB-LENGTH
CASUAL WATER	NO PENALTY, DROP WITHIN ONE CLUB-LENGTH
EMBEDDED BALL	NO PENALTY, DROP AS NEAR AS POSSIBLE (ON THE TEE, FAIRWAY, OR GREEN)

HANDS ON THE BALL

Proper Dropping, Lifting, and Placing

Losing a ball in the woods or splashing one in a pond are moments of human imperfection during an afternoon of golf. After which you must confront the consequences of your error. One entire section of the rules, titled Relief Situations and Procedure, is devoted to correcting the error and making reparations. In most cases, the rule instructs us, after a penalty of one or more strokes, to drop a new ball and resume play, sadder but wiser.

The procedure for dropping a ball is simple, but it must be followed carefully. Stand up straight, hold the ball at shoulder height,

CORRECT WAY TO DROP

RULE

20

WRONG

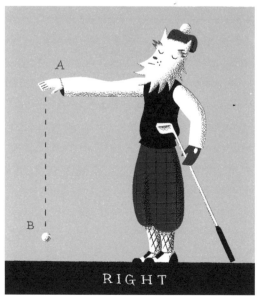

RIGHT

extend your arm all the way out (either in front of you or to your side), and release the ball from your hand. No flipping or throwing is permitted. You can position yourself so that your drop might find a nice lie—as long as your ball is still within the specified one or two club-lengths from the trouble spot that you're trying to escape. Though it may seem obvious, you are the only person who can drop your ball. You cannot have your caddie, your partner, or anybody else drop for you.

Watching old tournament footage on cable television, you may notice a player from the 1940s and 1950s, like Cary Middlecoff or Patty Berg, dropping a ball over a shoulder to resume play. But that bit of peekaboo has been out of the rule book for years. Today, the physical act of dropping a ball to resume play calls merely for the golfer to stretch out his arm in front of him or to the side. There's not much to improve on here, so you don't need to develop a special technique for dropping.

What's a bit more complex is determining exactly where to drop. In general, you will need to drop within either one or two club-lengths from the nearest spot of relief, depending on the situation. To measure out the parameters of your drop area, first mark with a tee or coin the nearest possible spot that is free from the problem area that you are trying to avoid. For instance, if your ball landed in a white-lined area of ground under repair, the nearest point of relief would be a spot on the ground just outside of the white line. Make sure this spot is not any nearer to the hole than your original lie.

Next, place your club on the ground extending out from the marker. Repeat this again if you need to drop within two club-lengths. Think of this club-length distance as being the radius of a circle; if you were to keep one end of the club planted on the nearest spot of relief and swing the other end to the left or right, you would form an imaginary circle. Half of this circle would be nearer to the hole than the nearest point of relief, and you cannot drop in this portion. The other half of the circle is the area where you can drop.

Looking through the section of the rule book that covers drops, Rule 20, Lifting, Dropping

PLACE A MARKER (A) BEFORE LIFTING YOUR BALL, MEASURE ONE OR TWO CLUB-LENGTHS FROM THE MARKER, BUT NOT NEARER THE HOLE.

and Placing, you would think a dropped ball could wander into trouble as easily as one that's been struck with a driver. The rule writers go to great lengths discussing the various mishaps that can occur once a ball tumbles from the player's hand. Fortunately, most drops turn out just fine. However, here are some of the ways they can go wrong: A dropped ball can roll back into the condition from which relief is being taken. It can roll more than two club-lengths from where it hits the ground. It can roll out of bounds. It can bounce and hit you on the leg or foot. Or, it can roll and come to rest closer to the hole than its original position. There is no cause for worry, though; in any of these cases, you simply re-drop without penalty. If the re-drop doesn't work, you can resort to placing the mischievous ball by hand. To do that, simply crouch down, pick up the ball, and place it where it last fell from your hand.

The first few times you take a drop may be enjoyable—whether you're willing to admit it or not. The act of dropping has a ceremonial feel to it. The procedure is especially pleasant in cases of ground under repair, casual water or the like, in which you are gaining your relief without penalty. Even in the scruffy patch of rough behind a pond after taking a penalty stroke, however, executing the drop is a bit of a consolation.

Dropping, if you think about it, is intended to simulate the ball's return to earth following a golf shot. We don't get to control our lie following a normal shot; therefore, we should not be given an opportunity to carefully place the ball following some mishap. So, as we drop the ball from shoulder height and watch it bounce and roll we are meant to be reminded of how the ball behaves when it drops from the sky.

However, there are other situations, both on and off the green, that call for a more precise action—lifting and placing the ball, instead of dropping it. In these situations, you find your ball within bounds, on a decent lie, and basically playable, but for some reason you need to lift it before making your shot. To put it back in play, there's no reason to drop since the original lie is fine. Also, the rules don't want you to improve your lie by dropping it elsewhere; the point is to preserve the original lie.

To imagine one such situation, say you tee off with another player and both of your shots veer toward the same patch of fairway that's obscured from view by some trees. When you reach the patch, there is confusion about whose ball is whose. It's perfectly legal, when this question arises, to lift and examine each ball's markings (under Rule 12-2, Identifying Ball). Of course, this means you need to have marked your ball somehow before starting

"A BALL INCORRECTLY SUBSTITUTED, DROPPED OR PLACED IN A WRONG PLACE...BUT NOT PLAYED MAY BE LIFTED, WITHOUT PENALTY, AND THE PLAYER SHALL PROCEED CORRECTLY."
—RULE 20-6

so that you can positively identify it. You cannot, however, pick up a ball in a hazard for
the purpose of identification.

With any instance of lifting and placing, you
must follow a strict procedure for marking
your ball Start by announcing your intentions
to a competing player, or to others in your
group. With the other player observing, mark
the ball's spot on the course before lifting. To
do this, use a ball marker, a coin, or any small
object that is handy, so that you will know
exactly where to put the ball back when
you're ready to do so. After you have picked
up the ball you may clean it. Then with the
other player watching, place the ball on its
marked spot.

In general, cleaning your ball is allowed, but
you can clean it only to the extent necessary
to identify it. On the other hand, if you have
to lift a ball in the process of recovering it
from some sort of unusual obstacle, like an
immovable obstruction or ground under
repair, or if it's embedded in the fairway, you
are allowed to clean it completely. The general operating principle is that, unless you've

run into some unintended obstacle, the rules want you to play your ball—up until you get to the green—in whatever state it may be, dirty or spotless. So, if you hook your shot into an area off to the side of the fairway that's full of moist earth that clings to your ball, you can't clean all of it off. Hitting a muddy ball in this case is part of the penalty you face for having hooked it.

"THE RESPON-
SIBILITY FOR
PLAYING THE
PROPER BALL
RESTS WITH
THE PLAYER."
—RULE 12-2

When you get to the green, however, the rules prefer cleanliness. So, it's a different story. You can clean the ball anywhere on the putting surface. Also, you don't drop on the green; you place. When you consider that the purpose of dropping is to re-create the randomness of a ball landing on a varied surface, there's no point in re-creating this randomness on the smoother surface of the green. So, when you mark and lift on the green, you return the ball to its spot by simply placing it there. We'll talk more about the rules on the green in Chapter 7.

There are a few other instances when you need to place a ball back in its previous spot. For example, if you're on steep ground in the rough or on the fairway and your ball moves after you address it, you would have to count a penalty stroke and place the ball back where it moved from (see Rule 18-2b). Or, if you're clearing loose impediments near the ball and happen to make it move, you also count a penalty stroke and place it back.

If, for some reason, you discover that you have mistakenly dropped or placed a ball at a time you were not supposed to, the rules go easy on you. As long as you have not gone ahead and hit, you are not in trouble. Rule 20-6 allows you to correct the error without penalty, going back to the place where you were before you dropped or placed and then proceeding correctly.

On the green, then, if you mark and lift your ball using a dull penny, then mistakenly place that ball down in front of some other player's dull penny, pocketing the marker, don't worry. As long as no one plays the ball, you can lift your ball from its wrong spot without penalty and put it on the correct spot. You should put the other player's marker back as close as possible to its original spot.

SITUATION	DROP OR PLACE	PENALTY STROKE INVOLVED?	RULE
IDENTIFYING BALL OUTSIDE HAZARD	PLACE	NO	12-2
EXAMINING BALL FOR DAMAGE	PLACE	NO	5-3
BALL MOVED DUE TO YOUR ADDRESS (OUTSIDE OF TEE-ING GROUND)	PLACE	YES	18-2
BALL MOVED DUE TO CLEARING IMPEDIMENTS THROUGH THE GREEN	PLACE	YES	18-2
BALL MOVED DUE TO CLEARING IMPEDIMENTS ON THE GREEN	PLACE	NO	18-2
BALL MOVED TO AVOID OTHER'S LINE OF PUTT	PLACE	NO	18-2
WATER HAZARD	DROP	YES	26-1
LATERAL HAZARD	DROP	YES	26-1
GROUND UNDER REPAIR/CASUAL WATER	DROP	NO	25-1
IMMOVABLE OBSTRUCTIONS	DROP	NO	24-2
UNPLAYABLE LIE	DROP	YES	28
EMBEDDED BALL	DROP	NO	25-2

CHAPTER FIVE

PULLING BACK GRASSES   TIME LIMIT ON SEARCHING
MOVING YOUR BALL DURING THE SEARCH
IDENTIFYING YOUR BALL AFTER THE SEARCH
PLAYING THE WRONG BALL

THE RECOVERY MISSION

Finding Your Ball

Standing in the fairway and getting set to launch a 3-wood shot to a distant green, a golfer sometimes slips into the heroic mode of a fighter pilot. A target is chosen and take-off awaits. But, when your ball departs from its direct route to the green, you find your-self performing a search-and-recovery mis-sion instead. First, you have to find your ball—whether it's lying among tall grasses, mixed in with pinecones, or hidden under leaves—then, you have to figure out how to get back to the fairway. If you have a tenden-cy to hit stray shots, keep a keen eye on the ball after it's struck so that you'll be better prepared to look for it when you reach its vicinity. After this point, let the rules guide you through the treacherous territory.

Rule 12, Searching for and Identifying Ball, allows you to bend any natural feature of the course that might be hiding your ball. So, you can pull back grasses and reeds in hope that they will reveal your ball. But be careful not to alter anything that might improve your shot. For instance, if there are many low-hanging branches surrounding the search

RIGHT   WRONG

area, you can part them to look for the ball. But, you can't twist them back or break them off to give yourself a clearer view of the green or fairway when you do find your ball. Doing anything like this to improve your hitting area leads to a two-stroke penalty. It's a good idea not to break off or deform trees or other natural growing things on the course even when it doesn't affect your shot. It's not a rules infraction, it's just bad etiquette.

"A BALL IS LOST IF IT IS·NOT FOUND OR IDENTIFIED AS HIS BY THE PLAYER WITHIN FIVE MINUTES AFTER THE PLAYER'S SIDE...HAVE BEGUN TO SEARCH FOR IT."
— DEFINITIONS

During your lost-ball search don't get so involved that you also lose track of time. The other members of your foursome won't appreciate that and neither will the rules. There is a five-minute time limit on any search, beginning from the time you start looking. If you exceed this, your ball is deemed officially missing in action—a lost ball. You are assessed stroke and distance; you must return to your last hitting spot and proceed with a one-stroke penalty. That is, if you haven't had the foresight to hit a provisional ball.

You must also be careful where you step. In the junglelike areas that hide your ball, check the ground before you put your foot down. Keep your eyes busily scanning left, right, and forward at all times. You never know what may be lurking just under your heel. For instance, your own ball may come up and bite you: If you, your partner, or your caddie step on, kick, or otherwise disturb your ball, Rule 18, Ball at Rest Moved, gives you one penalty stroke. Also be wary of picking up any natural objects that are in your way; a twig could turn out to be a loose root that reaches up next to your ball.

DO NOT DISTURB YOUR BALL DURING SEARCH

RULE
18

ONE-STROKE PENALTY FOR DISTURBING
YOUR BALL DURING SEARCH

For honest golfers, this constitutes a "sloppiness penalty." Many golfers judge this rule uncharitable and even unreasonable when they first hear of it. When they are told the rule also calls for the accidentally dislodged ball to be replaced in its original position, they are all the more prone to wonder why the replacement can't simply be free of penalty in every case—it is an honest mistake and all's forgiven.

To understand the logic, you must imagine golf without this rule: Visualize feet roaming through the rough while the owner of those feet seems to gaze absently skyward; visualize a ball accidentally dislodged from its buried lie—oops— then "re-placed" on a nice, fluffy lie just an inch or two away. The line, at these moments, between accident and unconscious but willful blunder, is simply too blurred to do without this rule. To reinforce the self-benefiting nature of such accidents, Rule 18 discriminates between the ball you might kick into an advantageous position and the ball an opponent might kick into that same position. When the opponent does the kicking, no one is assessed a penalty. The ball is just placed back in its original lie. You are also assessed no penalty when the ball played by your opponent that you accidentally move is in a hazard, ground under repair, or casual water.

When you do discover something that looks like your ball, you must then be able to positively identify it. Here's where a lot of golfers run into trouble. Though most amateur players love to imitate certain practices of the pros—like pulling off one's glove as a prelude to a putt, or placing lead tape on your iron or gauze on your grip—for some reason amateur players often neglect the pros' invariable practice of marking the ball so it can be identified. The rules do not require this, but they do strongly recommend it (in Rule 12-2). Being able to identify your ball in play is critically important to playing a match or to recording a valid score, but most average golfers don't usually take out the waterproof pen and ink their dimples. The primary reason is that most players have never suffered serious consequences due to an unidentifiable ball. Or perhaps it is more accurate to say that most have never *allowed* themselves to suffer these consequences.

"IF DURING A SEARCH FOR A PLAYER'S BALL, THE BALL IS *MOVED* BY AN OPPONENT, HIS *CADDIE* OR HIS *EQUIPMENT*, NO PENALTY IS INCURRED AND THE PLAYER SHALL REPLACE THE BALL."
—RULE 18-3A

"IF, OTHER THAN DURING SEARCH FOR A BALL, THE BALL IS TOUCHED OR *MOVED* BY AN OPPONENT... THE OPPONENT SHALL INCUR A PENALTY STROKE."
—RULE 18-3B

To understand the importance of marking your ball, imagine two beautiful drives that split the fairway then roll to a spot not visible from the tee, coming to rest within a few feet of each other. The players who hit these drives go to check which is which and find that the two balls are identical. Same brand, same printed number and no other feature or imprint that would tell them apart. A glance at Rule 27 reminds us that a ball is lost if it is not identified within five minutes of the time when a search has commenced.

In this case, a mere five seconds is all it takes for grim reality to set in—neither ball is strictly identifiable, so neither ball is identified, and so both are lost. The two might as well have disappeared into thin air. In tournament play, the golfers who hit them would be headed back to the tee, cursing and lamenting, to play their third strokes. In social golf, even with a wager involved, one player or the other will usually point out some nonexistent scratch that allows the question to be settled, though this is the wrong way out.

There's another reason you should make a

habit of identifying your ball. When you hit into treacherous territory, don't think you're the only one to have found this hideaway. Chances are great that others before you have abandoned balls in the same area. So it's very possible that you could find someone else's ball by mistake.

And, remember, the more arduous the search, the less you will be inclined to carefully inspect the ball to make sure it's yours. Often, a player will be so relieved at finding anything round as the time limit is reached that he or she will forget to double-check the brand and handmade markings of the ball. Rule 12-2 allows you to lift, inspect, and replace a ball in order to identify it on any point of the course except in a hazard (see Chapter 4). This removes any excuse for playing a wrong ball. It's a sickening feeling to get up to the green, lay down that penny behind the ball you just hit, and find that it isn't your ball at all. In such a case, you must retrace your steps and start searching all over again under Rule 15, Wrong Ball, taking a

In match play, you lose the hole. Don't hit a ball unless you're sure it's yours.

EXPLORATORY EXPEDITION CHECKLIST

RULES

12-2
MARK ANY BALL BEFORE USING IT TO PLAY
SO YOU CAN IDENTIFY IT.

WATCH YOUR BALL'S FLIGHT PATH AND
LANDING AREA CAREFULLY.

12-1
DURING THE SEARCH, DON'T ALTER ANY
COURSE FEATURES THAT COULD IMPROVE
YOUR SHOT.

18
WATCH WHERE YOU STEP TO AVOID
DISTURBING THE BALL.

27
REMEMBER THE FIVE-MINUTE SEARCH LIMIT.

12-2
CHECK THAT THE BALL YOU'VE FOUND
IS IN FACT YOURS.

**SECTION I:
ETIQUETTE**
RESPECT THE LANDSCAPE AND ITS
LIVING FEATURES.

JUST DESERTS

Escaping the Bunker

Think about how bunkers often surround or protect the green like a moat around a medieval castle. Though there is no penalty stroke for landing in a bunker (sometimes still referred to as a sand trap), escaping one almost always adds at least a stroke to your score. So remember that when you hit into a bunker, you have entered a zone that is designed to represent a challenge. The rules that govern bunker behavior are written to ensure that this challenge remains intact.

At any point on the fairway or on the green, you are free to examine your lie. You may also place your club behind the ball before you swing—a process called grounding your club—in order to calculate the nature of the shot or merely to gain confidence. If you wish to get more extensive geological information, you can also touch the ground with your hands to determine the consistency of the grass under your ball. You can even experimentally brush your club on the ground near your ball before making your stroke. These are all preliminaries to a golf swing that most players take for granted.

NO GROUNDING BEFORE SWING

INCORRECT

CORRECT

HITTING IN THE SAND

However, in the bunker you cannot perform any of them. You cannot touch the ground in a bunker with either your hands or your club. There can be no grounding of the club before you swing, according to Rule 13-4, Ball in Hazard. When you hit, the only element your club touches before striking the ball is thin air. These restrictions are the same that apply if you are hitting from within a water hazard. Both bunkers and water hazards are treated equally in this respect, under the term *hazards* in the rule book.

Of course there are logical exceptions to these strictures. If your ball has found the steep face of a deep bunker, and you feel yourself slipping as you prepare to hit, it's okay if you stick your club or hand into the sand to keep from falling. There's no penalty. Likewise if your hand touches the sand as you're removing or replacing a man-made object—an obstruction—that someone's left in the bunker. This could be an object like a candy wrapper, for example, that someone has discarded, or the rake used to smooth the bunker and that often remains inside it. And, while you're not supposed to touch the sand with your club, there's no problem if it touches a natural part of the course outside of the bunker during your swing. So don't worry if your club clips the high fairway grass when playing near the bunker's edge.

The most common way that golfers determine the density of the sand in a bunker without risking a penalty for testing the condition of the hazard is to wiggle their feet in the sand to establish a stance before hitting. This gives them some idea of how hard and clumpy or soft and fine the sand is. It comes as a gift, with no penalty.

"BEFORE MAK-
ING A *STROKE*
AT A BALL
WHICH IS IN A
HAZARD, THE
PLAYER SHALL
NOT TOUCH OR
MOVE A *LOOSE
IMPEDIMENT*
LYING IN OR
TOUCHING
THE *HAZARD*."
—RULE 13-4

Sometimes bunkers are not exclusively sand-filled; you may also find pebbles and stones, or leaves and pinecones that have naturally accumulated in them. Though you could do so elsewhere on the course, you cannot remove loose impediments in a bunker (under Rule 12-1). Remember that the purpose of a bunker is to be especially constricting. Even if there's a fairway divot next to your ball in the bunker, you get no relief. As long as it's a natural impediment, the rules expect you to play the ball just as it lies in the bunker.

But, what if the bunker is filled with a pile of leaves and you can't even see your ball? In such a case, you can brush away only as much of the leaves as needed to reveal your ball's location. If you remove more than what's necessary to see the ball, then you must re-cover the ball partly with the leaves. But there is no penalty for this mistake. There is also no penalty if you move

MOVE AWAY ONLY AS MUCH OF THE LEAVES AS NEEDED TO REVEAL YOUR BALL'S LOCATION

the ball in this process, but you must place it back in its original lie.

If you are really discouraged by your ball's lie beneath the sand or leaves, there is one somewhat extreme option available to you, as it always is at any point on the course: declaring your ball unplayable. You can return to the last spot from which you hit and take a penalty stroke, or you can drop with a penalty according to the unplayable rule's drop stipulations. The catch is that if you decide to drop, you must stay within the bunker. There's no easy way out.

When you do find a ball after brushing away some leaves in this type of situation, you may well wonder if it is truly your ball and not someone else's also lost in the leaf pile. Elsewhere on the course you would reach down and pick up the ball to identify it. Again, normal rights do not apply in a bunker. You cannot lift to identify your ball in a bunker.

Well, what if you hit someone else's ball? It's not a problem; the rules do not penalize you for hitting a wrong ball from a bunker. If you hit a ball from a bunker onto the green, get up to the green and then see it is not your ball, you are not penalized. In any other instance, a two-stroke penalty would be demanded for hitting a wrong ball. But when a bunker's involved, you go back to the bunker and play your correct ball from there. If the wrong ball you hit belongs to someone you're playing with, that player must put that ball back as near as possible to its original lie in the bunker (under Rule 15-3). If the wrong ball you hit turns out to be a ball someone had abandoned before your group got to this hole, you can just pocket it.

After you've found and hit the correct ball out of the bunker, it's likely you've made something of a mess of the bunker's sand, leaving behind your foot tracks and club marks. This leads to a point in bunker play where the rules and etiquette intersect. Golfers who hit into a bunker after you do should not have to deal with the added hardship of having their ball land in the impression your ball, feet, or swing make. Before you leave the area, you need to

"BEFORE LEAVING A *BUNKER*, A PLAYER SHOULD CAREFULLY FILL UP AND SMOOTH OVER ALL HOLES AND FOOTPRINTS MADE BY HIM."— CARE OF THE COURSE

smooth the bunker by pulling the course-provided rake across the sand that you disturbed. But, remember never to do this before you have taken your shot out of the bunker. If you let overzealous tidiness take over and rake before hitting, you incur a penalty of two strokes (or a loss of hole in match play), since this act could be construed as an effort at improving your lie.

Though the rules may seem harsh in their treatment of loose impediments within a bunker, they are not so bad when it comes to an artificial object—what the rules term an obstruction—in a bunker (under Rule 24). The most common obstruction you would find in a bunker is the rake. Some courses encourage you to leave the rake in the bunker after using it (to keep it out of the way of mowers), while other courses prefer that you lay it outside the bunker. In any case, if your ball lands near the rake you may pick the rake up and move it elsewhere with no penalty. If your ball moves in the process, there is also no penalty; just place it back as closely as possible to its original spot. In the rare situation in which your ball lands near an obstruction that is immovable—a piece of landscaping equipment, for example—you can drop within one club-length but not closer to the hole, with no penalty. Of course, you must stay within the bunker.

One more rare situation some course designers create is grassy spots within bunkers. Don't let these emerald islands discourage you: They are not considered part of the bunker. So, if your ball lands on one, you are allowed to ground your club.

If you encounter abnormal conditions in a bunker, which can be either ground under repair or casual water (Rule 25-1), you drop for relief within the bunker as close as possible to the trouble area but not nearer the hole. There is no penalty for this. You have a second option if casual water completely floods the bunker: You take a penalty stroke, imagine a line extending from the hole through the point at which your ball landed in the bunker, and then drop at any point behind the bunker as long as it's along the imagined line. When abnormal conditions like these occur in a bunker, the rules want to give you relief since these are unintended conditions. But, the rules do not want to give relief from the bunker itself. Your ball would have landed in the bunker whether the condition existed or not, so naturally there is no free ticket out of the bunker.

RULES TO REMEMBER: IF BY SAND

RULE

13-4 YOU CAN'T GROUND YOUR CLUB IN A BUNKER.

12-1 YOU CAN'T REMOVE LOOSE IMPEDIMENTS, EXCEPT JUST ENOUGH TO SEE YOUR BALL.

24-1 YOU CAN REMOVE OBSTRUCTIONS, LIKE CANDY WRAPPERS, OR A RAKE.

12-2 YOU CAN'T LIFT TO IDENTIFY (BUT THERE IS NO PENALTY FOR HITTING A WRONG BALL).

24-2 **25-1** YOU CAN TAKE THE USUAL FREE RELIEF FOR IMMOVABLE OBSTRUCTIONS OR ABNORMAL CONDITIONS, BUT MUST STAY WITHIN BUNKER.

ON THE GREEN

*Where Rules and
Etiquette Meet*

The putting surface is golf's high court,
where the good and the bad sportsman
are judged. Rule 16, The Putting Green, is
perhaps the only Rules of Golf passage in
which what a player is allowed to do (etiquette responsibility) gets nearly as much
attention as what he is forbidden to do
(rules responsibility).

The first question of politeness comes in
deciding who should hit first. Everyone in the
group is gathered closely around the green
waiting to proceed. The admirably courteous
golfers will ask whose turn it is. According to

Rule 10-2, Order of Play, the player whose ball is farthest away from the hole is the one to go first. This is important to remember since many commonly think that it is the player farthest from the *green* who is up. They think the point is to first get everyone on the green and then worry about who is away. In some cases a player on the green could actually be farther from the hole than someone on the fringe or in the rough. It's sheer distance that counts in order of play, not whether or not you're on the green.

"IF TWO OR MORE BALLS ARE EQUIDISTANT FROM THE *HOLE*, THE BALL TO BE PLAYED FIRST SHOULD BE DECIDED BY LOT."—RULE 10-2B

Once you reach the green, Rule 16 comes in with a general prohibition against touching the line of a putt, which is defined as the path that a ball on the green takes in order to get to the hole. Examining the line of your putt is the first thing you'll do on the green. Some do this by simply standing and looking down and out at the contours of the green to determine distance, speed, and direction. Others follow the procedure that pros on TV take: They crouch behind the ball, judging factors such as break, grain, and surface of the green. Whichever way you choose, it's important that in the process

STEPPING ON OR ALTERING THE PART OF THE GREEN THAT LIES ON THE LINE THAT CONNECTS YOUR BALL AND THE HOLE IS PROHIBITED

you do not step on or otherwise alter the part of the green that lies along the imaginary line that connects your ball and the hole. If you do touch any point on this line, others could consider it an attempt at unfairly improving your shot, an attempt at gaining an unfair advantage.

However, the same rule goes on to recite a litany of exceptions—times when it's okay to touch the line of putt. There's no penalty when you're doing any of the following: placing a marker down and lifting your ball;

measuring to see who is farthest away from the hole; brushing away debris; repairing old hole plugs or ball marks; or picking up clubs or the flagstick if someone has laid them in your way. We'll go over each of these procedures individually.

You may believe that there is a section of the rules that forbids you from stepping on another player's line of putt. Since the rules prevent you from interfering with your own path to the hole, you would think they would prevent you from interfering with

**GOOD GOLF
ETIQUETTE**

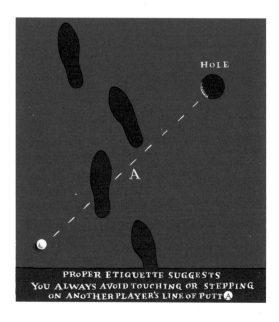

HOLE

A

PROPER ETIQUETTE SUGGESTS
YOU ALWAYS AVOID TOUCHING OR STEPPING
ON ANOTHER PLAYER'S LINE OF PUTT Ⓐ

someone else's as well. However, you won't find any such prohibition. That stipulation is part of the game's unwritten code of etiquette, not its formal rules. It's no less important though. You should always avoid touching or stepping on another player's line of putt. Whether the effect would be positive or negative, you would be exerting some influence on how the other player's putt would roll, and no one wants that.

There is one small act of golf etiquette on the putting green that can get you into a rules breach if you aren't careful. At any time, a player is given the opportunity on the green to lift and clean the ball, placing a marker in its place. Elsewhere on the course you can clean your ball only when you have lifted it for another purpose, but here you have permission to lift and clean. You also might lift your ball and mark its place if it seems to interfere with another player's line of putt. (By the way, this is true anywhere on the course—you can lift and mark your ball if another player considers it to be interfering with his or her shot.)

"ANY PLAYER MAY HAVE ANY OTHER BALL LIFTED IF HE CONSIDERS THAT THE BALL MIGHT INTERFERE WITH HIS PLAY."
—RULE 22

In any case, you should look to see whether your marker itself interferes with another player's putting line, or their stance. If it does, make sure you proceed according to the following marking, lifting, and replacing routine in a strict, step-by-step manner, both when you lift the ball and when you go to re-place it: 1) Place the marker behind the ball. Lift the ball and pocket it. 2)Next, select a nearby tree or bush toward which you will move the marker out of the way. Place the heel of your putter beside the marker and, pointing the toe of the putter at the select-

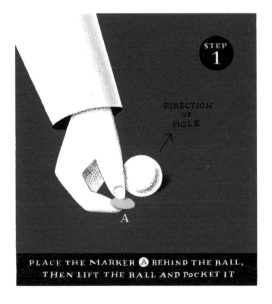

STEP
1

DIRECTION
OF
HOLE

A

PLACE THE MARKER Ⓐ BEHIND THE BALL,
THEN LIFT THE BALL AND POCKET IT

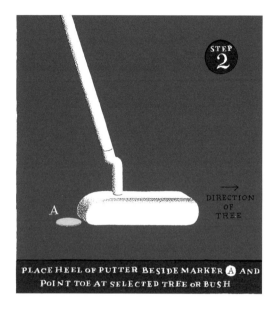

STEP
2

A

→
DIRECTION
OF
TREE

PLACE HEEL OF PUTTER BESIDE MARKER **A** AND
POINT TOE AT SELECTED TREE OR BUSH

SIX STEPS TO PROPERLY LIFT AND
REPLACE YOUR BALL ON THE GREEN

RULE
16-1B

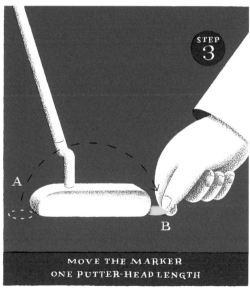

STEP
3

A

B

MOVE THE MARKER
ONE PUTTER-HEAD LENGTH

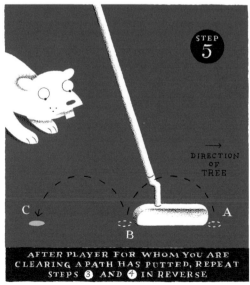

DIRECTION OF HOLE

TAKE THE BALL FROM YOUR POCKET AND PLACE IT IN FRONT OF MARKER

SIX STEPS TO PROPERLY LIFT AND REPLACE YOUR BALL ON THE GREEN

RULE

6-1B

ed tree or bush, 3) measure one putter-head length away. 4)If necessary, measure out a second putter-head length, saying out loud, "Two putter-heads toward that last birch," or wherever you use as your point of reference. Then when you're out of the other player's way, place the marker down in the new spot.

When the player for whom you were clearing a path has putted, proceed as follows: 5) Put the toe of your putter at the marker aligning the putter with your point of reference, lift the marker, and place it at the putter's heel. If you were two putter-heads out, move the putter again and replace the marker again. Only when you're finished leapfrogging your marker over your putter-head do you 6) take the ball from your pocket and place it in front of the marker. If you don't put your marker down that last time, you add an inch or two to the length of the putt. More importantly, you run up against Rule 20-7, Playing from a Wrong Place, which results in a two-stroke penalty (or a loss of the hole during match play).

To the newer golfer, such obsessive care in the moving and replacing of ball markers may seem excessive. Why is it so important? Two reasons, the first of which is symbolic. The manner in which you lift, mark, and place your ball is taken by veteran golfers as a sign of your overall conscientiousness and rules abidance. Of all the little protocols we perform in golf, this one is the most visible and the most frequent, making it a natural indicator of the care you take in other, less-witnessed situations. The second reason for taking such care is simply to avoid forgetting that you have moved your marker, which is extremely easy to do, especially when other putts have been read, discussed, and struck before it's your turn again. Your partner's twisting thirty-foot par putt that rims the cup but fails to fall—and your resulting eagerness to sink your own putt—can easily disrupt your thinking enough that you forget having moved the marker over.

The green is intended to be an especially clean, well-groomed part of the course. If small natural objects such as leaves or pinecones—loose impediments, as the rules call them—are in your way, you are free to remove them. You can remove loose sand or soil on the green. But when clearing away these impediments, you must use your hand or your club; you cannot use anything else, not even a cap or a towel, to sweep them away. This may seem like a strange rule, but it is intended to keep activity on the green and the green's surface as natural as possible.

"A BALL IS *'HOLED'* WHEN IT IS AT REST WITHIN THE CIRCUMFERENCE OF THE *HOLE* AND ALL OF IT IS BELOW THE LEVEL OF THE LIP OF THE *HOLE*."
—RULE 16, DEFINITIONS

The putting surface is never perfect however, and you may find it in a poor state. In general, repairs are allowed only to damage made by incoming balls or to work undertaken by the maintenance crew when, after cutting a new hole, they fill in the prior hole with a 4 1/4-inch plug, or cylinder of turf. The tool that cuts and removes these plugs is sharp and precise, and the cylinder of turf that is returned to fill the existing cup hole usually goes in so cleanly that it can hardly be spotted, but sometimes, that plug withers in its new spot and creates a dead circle with a bumpy ridge around its perimeter. Rule 16-1c allows you to repair it, but poking and prying with tees or repair tools seldom does much good. The rule lets you try, but don't expect great results.

Before putting or hitting onto the green, players are also allowed to repair the imprint made on the green by any incoming ball, yours or someone else's. If, while performing the repair, you accidentally move your own ball or another's, there is no penalty. Just place the ball as near as possible to its original position, and play on.

The final greens-repair issue, which golfers have discussed for years, involves spike marks. Metal spikes are accused of creating impressions in the turf, which, however tiny, can alter the direction of a putt rolling slowly toward the cup. Technically, the rules do not allow you to repair such marks, and many who still prefer the metal spikes argue that a new rule allowing this kind of repair should be instituted. However, with the nearly universal switch to nonmetal spikes among amateur golfers, this argument has almost disappeared.

If your ball encounters a hindrance that's less common on the green—casual water or ground under repair, which are termed abnormal ground conditions—you are entitled to free relief. You can lift and *place* the ball (don't drop it) at the nearest possible point that is outside of the trouble area but not nearer the hole. If your ball encounters an immovable obstruction on the green, you take the same relief—placing the ball in the nearest clear spot, but no closer to the hole. If there's a movable obstruction, then you just move it out of the way.

The rules may ensure that you get a clear shot at the hole, but they are not intended to reduce the overall challenge of putting. The rules forbid any player from testing the speed and contour of the green by rolling a ball along the surface. You are also not allowed to take a croquet-style stance, with feet on either side of the line of the putt. Nor can you use a caddie or partner as your personal aiming specialist during your stroke. You may not have them stand behind the ball or on the other side of the hole and guide you through a correctly aimed stroke. But you may have them perform about 90 percent of this guidance service, as long as they are off to the side by the time you begin your stroke. If they do not move aside while you putt, you are penalized two strokes or, in match play, you lose the hole.

Once a golfer's behavior on the putting surface has been clarified by consulting Rule 16, you're ready to move on to Rule 17, which governs the flagstick. Rule 17, The Flagstick takes up nearly two full pages in the Rules of Golf. Here, in brief, are the fundamentals that underlie the rule's requirements.

A player within striking distance of the hole needs—and deserves—to know where the hole is. Therefore, courses install flagsticks and players expect the flagstick to mark the position of the hole. If you strike the flagstick with a shot from *off* the green, you can play your next shot without penalty from wherever the ball has come to rest (or pull the ball from the hole and accept congratulations). On the other hand, if you strike the flagstick with a stroke from on the green, you are assessed a two-stroke penalty or, in match play, loss of hole.

"THE '*FLAGSTICK*' SHALL BE CIRCULAR IN CROSS-SECTION." —RULE 17, DEFINITION

Attending the flagstick, or pin (the terms are used interchangeably), for another player is a widely esteemed act of golf etiquette. It assures that a putt from on the green does not hit the flagstick. Ask the other player what he or she would like you to do. If you are attending the flagstick, you stand beside the flagstick as your companion putts. As the ball rolls toward the hole, pull the flagstick out. Alternately you could remove the pin and place it off to the side— just make sure you place it well out of danger of anyone's hitting it with their putt. It is the player who hits the unattended flagstick, and not the player who places it, who is stiffly penalized if a putt hits the flagstick. If you're about to putt and you see a flagstick (or someone else's clubs) lying in your way, you are free to remove them yourself. Even if you step on the line of your putt in doing this, there is no penalty.

No discussion of the flagstick rule would be complete without addressing the most common point of confusion—even panic— involving the flagstick. It is the moment when a player who is about to putt or chip from just off the green looks up to see that someone is tending the pin—or is trotting over to remove the pin after the ball is in motion. "Don't tend it," the player will protest, "I'm off the green." Sometimes, the player who's chipping is upset that his or her plan to use the flagstick as a backstop has been foiled. Just as often, however, the player is panicked that this act will cost a penalty.

This fear is unfounded. You can have the

flagstick attended when playing any shot from any position. The relevant point is that tending the pin for someone who is off the green is unnecessary, since we are permitted to hit the flagstick (in the hole) with our shots from off the green. If there is indeed a rules breach here, the guilty party is the well-meaning person who unasked goes for the flag while the ball is in motion. Rule 17-2a penalizes any competing player who does this.

Someone may attend the flagstick for you if you're off the green and you can't see exactly where the hole is. The person can even hold the stick and walk toward you so that you're sure of the direction. However, the attending person must be standing by the hole at the time of your actual stroke.

Say you're hitting from the bottom of a hill on the fairway and you can see neither the green nor the flagstick nor the hole. Someone can help you just by standing near the front of the green, between you and the hole, to help you align your shot. However, here again, this person must

YOU CAN INDICATE LOCATION OF HOLE
BEFORE STROKE...

...BUT NOT WHILE SHOT IS BEING TAKEN

move away when you are actually ready to make the stroke.

Once the flagstick is out of the way and your ball approaches the hole, you may, once in a while, encounter a strange greens occurrence. The ball rolls to the very edge of the cup, and then hangs as if frozen over the hole, unsure if it will fall in or stay out. After you have hit this almost-perfect putt, you are allowed only enough time to walk at a normal pace to the hole and then ten seconds more to see if the ball will fall in (Rule 16-2, Ball Overhanging Hole). Warning: After ten seconds, the ball is deemed at rest and you should hit it immediately because if it falls in thereafter, the falling counts as a stroke plus you receive one penalty stroke to boot.

Keep this ruling in mind in a match when your *opponent's* ball remains poised on the lip of the hole. If you concede your opponent's putt before the ten-second waiting period is over and knock the ball away, you are in breach of Rule 1-2 (Exerting Influence on Ball) and can lose the hole.

"IF THE BALL RESTS AGAINST THE *FLAGSTICK* WHEN IT IS IN THE *HOLE*, THE PLAYER MAY MOVE OR REMOVE THE *FLAGSTICK* AND IF THE BALL FALLS INTO THE *HOLE*, THE PLAYER SHALL BE DEEMED TO HAVE *HOLED* OUT WITH HIS LAST *STROKE*."
—RULE 17-4

STAYING CLEAN ON THE GREEN

RULES

YOU CANNOT TOUCH OR STEP ON YOUR
OWN LINE OF PUTT.

16-1

YOU SHOULD NOT TOUCH OR STEP ON
ANYONE ELSE'S LINE OF PUTT.

**GOOD GOLF
ETIQUETTE**

YOU CAN LIFT AND CLEAN YOUR BALL
ANYWHERE ON THE GREEN AT ANY TIME.

16-1

CAREFULLY MARK AND LIFT YOUR BALL IF IT
INTERFERES WITH ANOTHER'S PUTT.

16-1

YOU CAN REMOVE LOOSE IMPEDIMENTS
INCLUDING LOOSE SAND AND SOIL ONLY
WITH HANDS OR CLUB.

23

YOU'RE ALLOWED TO REPAIR BALL MARKS
OR HOLE MARKS.

16-1

TAKE RELIEF FROM CASUAL WATER, GROUND
UNDER REPAIR, OR IMMOVABLE OBSTRUC-
TIONS BY PLACING THE BALL ON THE NEAREST
CLEAR SPOT BUT NOT CLOSER TO THE HOLE.

25-1

24-2

DON'T HIT THE FLAGSTICK WHEN PUTTING
ON THE GREEN (TWO-STROKE PENALTY).

17-3

ALWAYS ASK BEFORE ATTENDING THE
FLAGSTICK.

17-2

IF YOUR BALL HANGS AT THE HOLE'S EDGE,
WAIT NO MORE THAN TEN SECONDS BEFORE
TAPPING IT IN.

16-2

Be Prepared

Scouting the Course

As you become more familiar with the rules, or at least consult them before, during, or after a round, you begin to look at golf courses and individual holes differently. You still scan fairways and greens in search of an advantageous route to the cup as you always have, but you also begin to notice the rules ramifications of various land features, hazards, and man-made obstructions.

For example, on a heavily treed course, you will notice whether the woods are "clean" or knee-deep in fallen branches and undergrowth. Sooner or later someone in your group will hit a wayward tee shot toward the wooded area, bringing up the question of whether a provisional ball should be recommended. The basics of the provisional ball are covered in Chapter 2. The natural optimism of a foursome tends to gives rise to cheery responses like "We'll find that one" when an off-line drive slips from sight into the trees. But when you know the woods are not "clean," the smarter, more realistic advice is to suggest that the player tee up a provisional ball.

Let's look at another scenario. Standing on an elevated tee, you see a creek down the right side of the fairway marked as a lateral hazard by red stakes (or a painted red line). Nothing exceptional about that—if someone drives into that creek, they can fix on the point where the ball entered the hazard and drop within two club-lengths of that point (see Chapter 2).

But what if, close by the far bank of the creek, there are dense woods? Say someone in the group hits a long, slicing drive that seems to flirt with both the creek and the

The GOLFER'S CONUNDRUM:
LATERAL HAZARD RULE or LOST BALL RULE?
IN CASE IT IS LOST, HIT A PROVISIONAL BALL.

treeline and ends up in one or the other without anyone seeing where it landed. Is it lost in the woods or lost in the lateral water hazard? Everyone searches, unsuccessfully, until someone feels compelled to venture a forthright opinion as to which of the two eventualities occurred:

1) The ball is either lost in the creek and the player gets to drop alongside the entry point, playing his third (under lateral hazard rule), or

2) The ball is lost in the adjacent woods and the player has to go back to the tee to play his third shot (under the lost ball rule).

If this situation occurs on a course you're playing, keep an extra-sharp eye on the flight of the ball. You might even survey the foursome for first impressions and instinctive guesses on where the ball ended up. The purpose would be to prepare the group for what may be a frustrating search and an unsatisfying adjudication of events. It would be especially wise, on the tee, to utter a casual but confident appraisal like, "Hit a provisional, Steve, because if that ball isn't in the creek, then it's lost in the woods, and you don't want to come all the way back to re-tee. Play a provisional."

Course designers can sometimes be so inventive that they create unusual rules situations that you should be on the lookout for. For instance, if there is a pondlike water hazard just before the green, there might be a footbridge crossing it. If someone's ball lands on the bridge in the middle of the hazard, naturally it will bring up confusion:

BEST BRIDGE OPTION: PLAY IT AS IT LIES
NO PENALTY

RULE

13

Should this be treated as a water hazard, an obstruction, or a regular lie? Since it is an artificial construction and thus an obstruction, it seems that you should get free relief. You do not. But even if you could, the only place to drop would be in the water. Instead, you can proceed as you would if the ball had gone into the water: going back to your last hitting spot or dropping behind the hazard, counting one penalty stroke. However, your best option would be to simply hit it as it lies on the bridge's surface, with no penalty, and you would be able to ground your club in this case. As a group is teeing up, it is the prepared golfer who will notice that a bridge like this exists on a hole, and will mentally review the rules that would apply before anyone hits.

Another curious course situation involves water hazards as well. Say there is a lateral hazard stretching the length of the fairway. It's clearly marked with red stakes, but there is very little water in the water hazard; it's mostly just a muddy bank. The prepared golfer thinks ahead, what's the right proce-

BALL IN DRY WATER HAZARD: NO RELIEF FROM EMBEDDED BALL RULE, NO GROUNDING OF CLUB

dure if someone hits into this? The answer is to play it as it lies with no penalty; there's no need to get relief if the ball is playable. However, if the ball gets stuck in the mud, you can't act under the embedded-ball rule and lift and drop without penalty. You would have to try to hit it out in its embedded state. And remember that you cannot ground your club in a hazard.

What about when your ball is not embedded, but just the opposite—your ball is precariously perched somewhere, like on

RULE

18-2

DON'T ADDRESS THE BALL WHEN HITTING FROM A PRECARIOUS SPOT. IF IT MOVES, YOU INCUR A ONE-STROKE PENALTY.

top of a fluffy tuft of tall grass, or on the slope of a steep hill? This is another situation to look out for. Don't address the ball as usual in these instances because if you do, chances are high that the ball will get unsettled and roll a bit. If this happens, you are penalized one stroke. If you instead approach the spot carefully and then hit it in one fell swoop, you have better chances. When starting out on a hole, look around for these kinds of lies and remind yourself of this rule. This will help you resist the automatic urge to address the ball as usual in any lie.

Scanning the geography of the course to sniff out potential scrapes with the rules is effective only if you also know the geography of the rule book itself. How to navigate the rule book is the subject of the next chapter.

THE SNARE	THE SOLUTION	RULES
WOODS LITTERED WITH LEAVES AND DEAD BRANCHES	PROVISIONAL BALL	27-2
LATERAL HAZARD CLOSE TO WOODED AREA	BALL LOST, BALL IN WATER HAZARD	27 / 26-1
CASUAL WATER IN BUNKERS	CASUAL WATER	25-1
BLIND AREAS LOCATED IN THE FAIRWAY	WRONG BALL	15
UNMARKED PILES OF GRASS CUTTINGS	GROUND UNDER REPAIR	25-1

DETECTING A REAL CHEATER

Although most rule infractions are caused by ignorance rather than deceit, chances are that if you play enough golf you'll eventually run into a real cheater. But, you don't have to be a rules expert to realize another player is deliberately cheating. When playing a match or competing for some prize other than self-esteem, you will want to keep an eye out for the most common examples of unvarnished cheating, which are as follows:

A player who has not played a provisional ball and who takes one penalty stroke only when stroke and distance is called for.

Not reporting strokes taken in remote areas like woods or tall grass.

Kicking the ball to a better position in the rough—the notorious "foot mashie."

Surreptitiously dropping a ball in the woods or the rough when the original ball appears to be lost; or claiming that a newly discovered ball that has actually been lying in the rough for days or weeks is the original ball.

On balls lost in lengthy lateral water hazards, designating a point where the ball last crossed the margin that is far in advance of the logical spot. The deception may be a case of accidental overoptimism, but it's always best to be conservative in these cases of self-adjudication.

On short putts, dropping a ball marker and lifting the ball in one purposely sloppy motion that leaves the marker closer to the hole than it should be. The process can also be repeated during replacement of the ball, gaining even more precious inches.

A purposely poetic reading of who's away on the putting green in order to prompt another player to putt first and reveal details of line, surface, or break. Insist on a confirmation of who is farthest away from the hole.

MURKY WATERS

Navigating the Rule Book

Just as purchasing the best cookbooks won't make you an instant chef, zipping a rule book into your golf bag will not automatically teach you the proper courses of action when a rules issue arises. As many golfers have found, the rule book's handy size and its seemingly clear indexing system are deceptive. When a knotty situation presents itself, the conscientious player will pull out the rule book to look up a certain point for the first time, and immediately be plunged into a recital of definitions and terms that have evolved over two centuries.

MARK UP YOUR RULE BOOK FOR
EASY NAVIGATION

This is bound to create problems, mainly involving other players coming up from behind. In general, it's best not to pull out the rule book—or quote a rule—unless you are certain you can quickly find the specific point in question.

If you have first learned to navigate the geography of the rule book, you'll be in a better position to use it on the course. Start by buying several copies of the rule book. Put them in handy places. Keep one in your golf bag and another on your nightstand. Leaf through the book often to become familiar with its contents. Keep one copy by the television—so you can relate what you see during televised tournaments to the proper paragraph and clause of the rules. Once you are in the habit of quickly opening the book and looking something up, you won't feel intimidated by it.

Off the course, practice referring to the rule book by checking on only the simplest of questions. For example, what kind of relief can you get from a "no carts" sign? To solve the cart-sign question, you would need to be familiar enough with the rule book's definitions to know that the sign in question is considered an "obstruction" and to look in the Index under either "Obstruction" or "Interference." This would lead you to Rule 24-1 which states "a movable obstruction...may be removed...if the ball does not lie in or on the obstruction.... If the ball lies in or on the obstruction, the ball may be lifted, without penalty, and the obstruction removed." Then you would return the ball as near as possible to its original position.

In dispensing this kind of information, it would be a fine thing if you could do so from memory—all the way down to the rule's number, paragraph, and clause. But it might be more practical to take a highlighting pen and mark the pages and passages in the rule book that you refer to most often. You may feel a bit strange identifying your "favorite rules," but haven't you taken a highlighting marker to other textbooks you've owned? The rule makers are not planning to print smiley-face symbols in the rule book's margins, so the individual user is the one who has to mark up his one-dollar booklet with notes or color-codes that make reference to commonplace rules faster and easier.

Develop a system that is tailored to your own needs: Use blue, for example, to highlight rules your golf buddies most often misquote and disobey, and yellow to mark rules that apply to your home course's most disruptive features—power lines stretched high across the 15th hole; dunelike sand deposits that swallow golf balls but are not designated as hazards, and so on.

To make the reference process easier still, you could use the highlighting pen to mark the most commonly used index headings and page numbers in the back of the book. You will learn that looking up entries in the Contents and in the Index is sometimes a two- or three-step process. The rule book's organization has been a major focus of the governing bodies' revision work over the past few decades, and its current structure is very sound. Still, there are numerous passages that belong with equal logic to more than one subsection, making their final location something of an arbitrary decision. Highlighting the headings you most often look up will save you time in the long run.

In personalizing your pocket rule book with notes and highlight colors, feel free to make a single diagonal slash through passages that are foreign to the style and format of your golf game. Rule 32, for example, covers Bogey, Par and Stableford Competitions, oddball variants on standard scoring that seems to have drifted far out of fashion. These formats are still in use, of course, which means the rule book has to address them. But when you open your rule book to look up something basic and urgent, it is annoying to come upon the list of disqualification penalties that are particular to Stableford play.

Also cross out just about everything in Rule 6 (The Player) and Rule 7 (Practice)—sections that cover all the competitive niceties of formal tournament play, including signing an incorrect scorecard, practicing the day of a stroke-play tournament on the course hosting the tournament, and not missing your starting time. Most of us could mark a nice, diagonal line through these pages.

Then there are sections that deserve a wavy line down the entire margin to indicate unusual difficulty and complexity. Rule 26-2b is a good example, addressing the tangled web we weave by playing a ball from within the confines of a water hazard. Question: What happens if I play from within a water hazard and knock my already-moist ball out of bounds? One answer: I take one penalty stroke, then drop another ball on the same misbegotten spot. Another answer: take two penalty strokes and go back to the spot from which I hit into the hazard. Or, well, there are a couple of other equally depressing options. In marking up your rule book, you might choose to write in the margin of 26-2b: "Note to self: Don't play from within a water hazard!"

WHEN THE RULES SEND A PLAYER CROSS-COUNTRY:

The American Midwest is full of nine-hole courses built more or less by hand on the back acreage of a family farm. Nothing fancy, but the folks in town don't need a 72-hole megaplex to enjoy their Saturday golf. However, the sons and daughters who are brought up maintaining and playing these pastureland courses eventually do feel the need for some variations in the routing. On an evening when no one else is around they are known to start on, say, the third tee and negotiate an 850-yard, par-8 hole of their own devising, crossing three fairways and finishing on the 6th or 7th green.

Hardly the style of play recognized in the Rules of Golf, but there is a circumstance where the rules force a tournament golfer to proceed on a cross-country route. If you doubt this, then take another look at Rule 11-4 and Rule 11-5.

Rule 11-4a, which applies to match play only, reads as follows: "If a player, when starting a hole, plays a ball from outside the teeing ground, the opponent may immediately require the player to cancel the stroke so played and play a ball from within the teeing ground, without penalty." Now continue forward to Rule 11-5, Playing from Wrong Teeing Ground, which consists of a simple, one-sentence codicil: "The provisions of Rule 11-4 apply."

Here's what that means: Four golfers are playing a match on an unfamiliar course. They putt out on the 5th hole and three of them stop to buy sodas from the beverage wagon. The fourth player goes on ahead, arriving at what he believes to be the 6th tee. In fact he is on the 12th tee, which plays downhill from a clifflike elevation and runs in the opposite direction of number 6. As the mistaken player's drive plummets down the 12th fairway, the rest of the group arrives and points out his error.

At that point, the members of the opposing twosome "may immediately require" that the erroneous tee shot be canceled. The key word is "may." If the twosome is kind, they definitely will cancel the shot so the mistaken player can start again. But if they're feeling merciless, they can let the shot stand. This requires the misguided player to make his way back to the proper hole by whatever route seems most expedient, counting every cross-country stroke as he goes.

QUESTIONS TO ASK TO LOCATE
A SPECIFIC POINT IN THE RULE BOOK

ONE

IS THIS STROKE PLAY, OR MATCH PLAY?

TWO

WHERE ON THE COURSE—TEE, GREEN,
HAZARD, FAIRWAY, OR ROUGH—DOES
THE BALL UNDER DISCUSSION LIE?

THREE

WAS A BALL AT REST MOVED, OR A
BALL IN MOTION DEFLECTED OR
STOPPED? (IF SO, TURN TO RULES 18
AND 19.)

FOUR

IS RELIEF, AND THEREFORE A DROP,
GOING TO BE NEEDED (CHECK RULES
20-28)?

FIVE

DOES THIS INVOLVE A PLAYER'S EQUIP-
MENT? (RULES 4 AND 5 WOULD APPLY.)

DISCREET
KNOWLEDGE

*When to Speak and When
to Hold Your Peace*

Golf's myriad situations sometimes call for a player to speak up about a rules infraction, and sometimes to keep silent. At the heart of this decision is golf's code of etiquette. The rules don't go into much detail about golf etiquette. And what the book says comes only in the form of recommendations; there are no strict decrees and no penalties are applied. However, the topic of etiquette is paid a certain degree of deference by its position at the very beginning of the rule book. In one paragraph from this section, titled "Consideration for Other Players," the rules tell us: "No one should move, talk or stand close to or directly behind the ball or hole when a player is addressing the ball or making a stroke."

The passage doesn't mention anything about jingling coins in your pocket while some high-strung, rabbit-eared opponent is getting ready to hit a tee shot. Nor do the rules make any provision for the slippery six-foot putt that zooms forty feet past the hole after a clumsy member of your foursome drops his bag of clubs just as your putter is coming forward to tap the ball. There are some rules that are okay to ignore, depending on the situation and the group you're playing with.

Everyday golfers carry their own provision for the do-over. We treat unintentional slips and screw-ups as regrettable but not irrevocable. The person who caused the distraction is usually mortified and will insist the stroke be done over. Here, sportsmanship overcomes the rules and the spooked golfer usually accepts the offer. However, some golfers will always refuse such clemency, and it is not only useless but a further irritant to press the point.

Another etiquette-driven rules breach that happens on a regular basis takes place on the green: Someone stands astride or on the line of his or her own putt to avoid stepping on another player's line of putt. However, there's no good in calling this as a rules breach. To envision this scenario, imagine that a group's first putts have all been hit and the cup is surrounded by pennies and dimes. One player tiptoes over and sets his ball down. To be polite to his fellow players, he takes pains to avoid stepping on anyone else's line to the hole while he is making his putt. This may require an unorthodox stance—a stance that would be in breach of Rule 16-1e. The penalty would be two strokes, or loss of hole in match play. However, no one really should call out this kind of breach because the player's intent is clearly sporting and there is hardly an advantage in taking one of these awkward stances.

In weekend play there's also no need to be a stickler about exceeding the fourteen-club maximum. When the rule makers limited tournament golfers to fourteen clubs (thirteen plus a putter), it was a bold offensive against wanton excess in the equipment realm. Sometimes tournament golfers in the 1930s carried more than thirty clubs. Without Rule 4-4, we would have broken-back caddies and endless debates about which club to use on a particular shot. But outside of tournament play, it isn't good manners to count your fellow golfer's clubs and make noise about the fourteen-club rule. In most cases, a golfer only confuses himself by carrying around all those options.

Another rule that's okay to forget in specific instances of friendly play: Rule 8-1, Advice. Technically, when it comes to subjective issues such as club choice or game strategy, you are not supposed to give advice to or receive advice from anyone except your partner or caddie. However, if it's a casual game among friends and someone asks for a tip, you should feel free to help out. This is especially true if there is a particular oddity about the course with which only you are familiar. You might want to say for instance, "That hill is steeper than it looks—you might want an extra club."

"INFORMATION ON THE *RULES* OR ON MATTERS OF PUBLIC INFORMATION, SUCH AS THE POSITION OF *HAZARDS* OR THE *FLAGSTICK* ON THE *PUTTING GREEN*, IS NOT *ADVICE*."
—RULE 8, DEFINITIONS

Be careful though about giving unsolicited personal lessons, like "Keep your left arm straight," or "Try standing closer to the ball." Even beginners often do not want to hear this kind of advice since it can come off as condescension. Remember one of golf's greatest assets is its requirement that each player is responsible solely for his or her own game. If you're receiving unwanted advice like this, you might try to deflect it gently by saying, "You know, you're probably right, but sometimes the only way to learn something is to do it wrong a few times at first."

If there's a question concerning nonstrategic information—about the layout of a particular hole or the distances between tee and green—it's perfectly fine to talk about this with anyone on your side or on the competing side. The rules do not consider this to be "advice," since it is public information that everyone has a right to know. Questions about the rules themselves fall under this category as well.

Eventually, you will be called upon to chip in with your own take on a specific rules question. This can lead to a sticky situation when the golfer who's asking doesn't quite agree with your assessment. For instance, imagine you're playing in a corporate event on a new suburban course. One executive in your foursome drives into the woods left of the fairway, his ball bouncing off a homeowner's fence that abuts the course. The ball comes to rest along the fence line in a shallow dirt furrow that has no lining of asphalt or any other manufactured material.

Under the rules, this would either be treated as an integral part of the golf course (meaning you play your ball as it lies) or as an interference-causing obstruction from which you receive relief of no more than one club-length.

This is the assessment you give when the executive asks your opinion. You use the official language of the Rules of Golf, mixing in a few *um's* and *I guess's* to keep things casual. "Nahh," the executive rasps, looking in various directions and gesturing toward the crude runoff channel. "It's for drainage. I get a drop on the fairway."

IN MOST ROUNDS, DON'T QUOTE
THE RULES UNLESS ASKED

In all of the rule book, there is really no language that would allow such a dramatic woods-to-fairway relocation of the ball other than Rule 28, Ball Unplayable, which brings with it a penalty stroke. This executive, however, has no thought of assessing himself one. But when you're flouting the rules, you are a free bird. So out of the woods and over to the fairway this fellow goes, taking at least twenty strides through the pines before reaching safety.

In a situation like this, you feel like a do-gooder who has just attempted a citizen's arrest and has bungled it badly. There's no use in pressing the point or arguing; that would only increase the awkwardness. Just suck it in and hope that the gods of golf one day seek retribution on this rules flouter.

Even when a golfer who has inquired about a rules point takes what you've said to heart, you're likely to hear a patronizing response like, "Gee, a real rules expert." To deflect comments like that, issue a disclaimer: "Hardly . . . I just happen to know that one." You will surely be telling some shade of the truth. Always give rules advice in an evenhanded diplomatic tone. Even after you feel you've mastered the rules, don't dispense information with a know-it-all arrogance. You never know when a previously undetected clause will come back and get you.

Once you have built a great store of rules knowledge, it is your decision as to how and when to use it. For certain, knowing the rules makes watching live or televised tournaments more enjoyable. It also helps enormously in the decision-making and traffic-directing arbitration that keeps your group moving and keeps the marshal from having to ride by in his cart and deliver a warning.

What also happens when you bolster your rules knowledge is that you become more likely to call rules violations on yourself. The twig you picked up that turned out to be a root that disturbed the ground and caused your ball to move adds a stroke to your score. Knowing the traps and snares, you can more clearly see into your own soul. What you will sometimes find is that, having declared a penalty on yourself and reported it to your opponent in a match, the opponent will then try to cancel the declaration. Some will actually take offense at the idea that you expect them to attest to the penalty stroke. "What do you take me for," they will say, "some obsessed rules geek?" At which point you should mark the score (including your penalty stroke) and reflect on the fact that now you are truly a rules-abiding golfer.

DIPLOMATIC IMMUNITY: SOME IGNORABLE RULES IN CERTAIN SITUATIONS

RULE	SITUATION	OKAY TO IGNORE IF...
1-3	AGREEMENT TO WAIVE RULES	PLAYER DISTRACTED BY ANOTHER'S INCONSIDERATE NOISEMAKING
16-1E	STANDING ASTRIDE OR ON LINE OF PUTT	PLAYER IS TRYING TO AVOID DISTURBING ANOTHER'S LINE OF PUTT
4-4	MAXIMUM OF FOURTEEN CLUBS	IT'S JUST A CASUAL WEEKEND ROUND
10-2C	PLAYING OUT OF TURN	IT'S JUST A CASUAL WEEKEND ROUND
8-1	ADVICE	IT'S A FRIENDLY GAME, ESPECIALLY IF BEGINNERS ARE INVOLVED

I SAW IT ON TV

One of the great impediments to the spread of rules knowledge is the prevailing sense that only misanthropic individuals go to the trouble of studying their rule books. To learn the rules would be to somehow join their ranks. One important source of that belief is the television-watching rules maven who spots an apparent violation and calls tournament headquarters to report it. A check of the videotape and an interview with the player (and sometimes his or her caddy) ensues. Then retroactively the player is assessed a penalty that often means disqualification because the player, unaware of the breach, has signed an incorrect scorecard, the penalty for which is disqualification.

This display of rules knowledge is truly frustrating because it never seems to help the player in question. In "real-time" rules officiating, a member of the tournament committee or a staff official can arrive on the scene to provide information and interpretations that, in many cases, grant a player unpenalized relief. But the television viewer can't act fast enough to affect situations positively, which means the input is always misanthropic.

Having said that, however, there must have been occasions when a rules-savvy fan watching a televised tournament noticed something amiss, confirmed the breach in the rule book, called directory assistance to get the phone number to report the breach, then decided not to dial it. Knowing that the officials would be forced to act on this tip, the tipster withholds it. There is no requirement to make such a call—indeed, there is something decent about not making it.

CONTRIBUTORS AND ACKNOWLEDGMENTS

GREG CLARKE, who produced the illustrations for this book, lives in Thousand Oaks, California. His work has appeared in magazines, such as *Rolling Stone, The New Yorker, The Atlantic Monthly,* and *Time*; and in books published by Running Press and Simon & Schuster.

He is currently developing characters for The Getty Museum in Los Angeles. He has exhibited in New York, Los Angeles, and Tokyo.

THE CALLAWAY GOLFER wishes to acknowledge the following individuals for their contributions to this book:
William Black, Rye, New York; Mark Burris, Greensboro, North Carolina; Tori Graham, Pittsburgh, Pennsylvania; Don Jozwiak, Callaway Golf Company, Carlsbad, California; Robert S. Macdonald, Publisher of Flagstick Books, New York City; Clark Renner, Carlsbad, California, for reviewing the text.

Also, David Gould, Sandy Hook, Connecticut, for contributing to the development of the text;
Anthony Scheitinger, West Orange, New Jersey, for copy editing the text;
Melissa Yow, Bridgeport, Connecticut, for proof-reading the text;
Sally Heflin & The Artworks, New York City, for help in developing the illustrations.